Dinosaurs

Funny & Weird

Extinct Animals

By

P. T. Hersom

D1739323

This book is dedicated to my three year old boy Gabriel, who loves dinosaurs and helped me pick out the pictures while sitting on my lap. Ahrrr.....

Love ya, Gabriel!

Let's Talk About Dinosaurs

The word dinosaur means 'terrible lizard'. It was created by English paleontologist Richard Owen in 1842 and was implied to describe their remarkable size instead of their frightening appearance. Nevertheless, dinosaurs are not lizards. Rather, they are a different group of reptiles.

The largest dinosaurs were more than 120 feet long and 50 feet high. The sauropod was the biggest dinosaur. The tiniest dinosaurs were about the size of a chicken and were named mussaurus, meaning mouse lizard.

When Did Dinosaurs Live?

Dinosaur Fossils

From dinosaur fossils discovered throughout the globe, paleontologists (that is the name provided of a person who researches dinosaurs), have actually acquired evidence regarding when dinosaurs lived, exactly what they ate and just how huge they grew. Dinosaurs lived throughout the Mesozoic age, from 245 million to 65 million years ago. The Mesozoic age is separated into three periods: Triassic, Jurassic, and Cretaceous. These periods actually refer to the geological layers of the earth's crust or rock, which the dinosaur fossils were found in.

The oldest period known as the Triassic started 230 million years ago, the middle period known as the Jurassic ranged from 200 to 140 million years ago and the most recent period being the

Cretaceous, which ended 65 million years ago. That is, if you can consider 65 million years ago as being "recent".

Kinds of Dinosaurs

Dinosaurs were not all the same, they ate different things, some walked on two legs and others four. Some had feathers, while others had horns. Some had wings in which to soar, and some were scary like the T-Rex, that could roar!

Carnivores - Which means "meat eaters", they were called theropods and were the dinosaurs that had two legs.

Herbavores - Which means "plant eaters", they were called sauropods and were the dinosaurs that had four legs.

Flying and Water Dinosaurs - The dinosaurs that could fly or lived in the water were NOT actually dinosaurs. These creatures are called flying and water based reptiles, but lived during the same time the dinosaurs did.

Dinosaur Families

Paleontologists classify dinosaurs with similar characteristics into a genus or family group. Here are some of the weird and funny dinosaur families.

Duck-billed Dinosaur or Hadrosaurids – These dinosaurs had heads that look like a ducks.

Bone-headed Dinosaurs or Pachycephalosaurs – These dinosaurs have heads (skulls), up to 12 inches think.

Horned Dinosaur or Ceratopsians – These dinosaurs had horns on their faces and/or heads, and might remind you of an elephant or rhinoceros.

Plated Dinosaur or Stegosaurs – These dinosaurs are known by double rows of plates and/or spikes that run down their backs, plus the spikes at the end of their tails.

Armored Dinosaur or Ankylosaurs – These dinosaurs had hard, scaly body armor, as well as spikes and bony plates, and some had wicked clubs at the end of their tails.

Amargasaurus

How do I pronounce its name? ah-MAR-gah-SORE-us

What does its name mean? The Amarga lizard.

How big were they? 35 feet/10 meters long and weighed 5000 lbs/2268 kg

What did they like to eat? Plants.

Where did they live? In the forest of South America.

Tell Me More

When it comes to a sauropod, or large plant eating dinosaur, Amargasaurus was actually really small. Like most other sauropod dinosaurs, Amargasaurus had five toes on each of its four feet, with the biggest containing a large claw. This fairly slim plant eater had a row of sharp spines lining up its neck and back, the sole sauropod known to have evolved such an imposing trait.

Why did they possess such striking spines? Just like similarly equipped dinosaurs, there are various likelihoods: the spines may have discouraged predators, or they may have had a part in temperature regulation. Some paleontologists believe that they were blanketed by a thin flap of skin capable of dissipating heat, called a skin sail.

Amargasaurus inhabited the early Cretaceous period in a time when huge meat eating dinosaurs walked the earth. Its little size made it a target for those hunters. The spines or skin sails might have puzzled the predators; making them imagine Amargasaurus was bigger than they really were.

Baryonyx

How do I pronounce its name? bah-RYE-oh-nix

What does its name mean? The heavy claw.

How big were they? 31 feet/9.5 meters long, 9 feet/2.75 tall and weighed 5000 lbs/2268 kg

What did they like to eat? Animals and fish.

Where did they live? In England and Western Europe.

Tell Me More

Baryonyx is one of the strangest dinosaurs yet uncovered. This huge hunter, while a genuine dinosaur, also shared many characteristics with the crocodiles. Plus had enormous front claws, a long narrow skull and well muscled arms. Paleontologists have arrived at the stunning conclusion that this early Cretaceous theropod hunted riverbanks and lakebeds, spearing passing fish with its claws. In truth, the remains of prehistoric fish have been discovered in the belly of one Baryonyx fossil.

Baryonyx had one huge claw around 12 inches long which perhaps was used for both defense against enemies, in addition to a useful tool for hunting and fishing.

Beipiaosaurus

How do I pronounce its name? BAY-pee-ow-SORE-us

What does its name mean? The Beipiao lizard, Beipiao is a city in China.

How big were they? 7 feet/2.1 meters long and weighed 75 lbs/34 kg

What did they like to eat? Plants.

Where did they live? In the forest of Asia.

Tell Me More

Beipiaosaurus is one more of those strange dinosaurs from the Early Cretaceous period in the therizinosaur family: long clawed, pot bellied, two legged herbivorous theropods that appear to have been created from bits of other kinds of dinosaurs. Beipiaosaurus seems to have been smarter than its counterparts because of its larger sized skull, and it's the only therizinosaur verified to have downy feathers, though it's highly likely that others did too.

Euoplocephalus

How do I pronounce its name? YOU-oh-plo-SEFF-ah-luss

What does its name mean? The well armored head.

How big were they? 23 feet/7 meters long and weighed 4000 lbs/1814 kg

What did they like to eat? Plants.

Where did they live? In the forest of North America.

Tell Me More

Euoplocephalus was among the most common dinosaurs to inhabit the late Cretaceous period. Better than 40, almost whole skeletons have been discovered in the American west. Created like a tank, Euoplocephalus had spikes on the side of its head as well as extending along its armored back, and its eyelids had bony protrusions. Its rigid tail finished with a hammer, which it might have used to try and damage the legs of attackers, like the T-Rex.

Giganotosaurus

How do I pronounce its name? GEE-gah-NOTE-oh-SORE-us

What does its name mean? The giant southern lizard.

How big were they? 43 feet/13 meters long and weighed 17000 lbs/7700 kg

What did they like to eat? Animals.

Where did they live? In the marshland of South America.

Tell Me More

Living during the middle Cretaceous period this South American theropod was seriously gigantic, at 43 feet long and 8 1/2 tons slightly outweighing even the T-Rex. Giganotosaurus also seems to have had a more awesome armory at its disposal, including much larger arms with three clawed, grasping fingers on each hand and elevated spines running down the middle of its backside.

Although greater in size than the T. Rex, it didn't possess nearly the biting strength, being three times less powerful. However, Giganotosaurus did possess razor-sharp arrowhead shaped teeth, used for slicing through the thick hides of its prey. Its head on its own would have been bigger than many grownup human bodies, more than 5 feet long, implying that Giganotosaurus could possibly have devoured a caveman in a single chomp.

Hadrosaurus

How do I pronounce its name? Had-roe-sore-uss

What does its name mean? The sturdy lizard.

How big were they? 33 feet/10 meters long and weighed 6000 lbs/3000 kg

What did they like to eat? Plants.

Where did they live? In the forest of North America.

Tell Me More

Hadrosaurus was first discovered in 1838 making it one of the very first dinosaurs to be named in North America. Living during the late Cretaceous period, this herbivore is part of the duck-billed dinosaur family because of its large, broad, flat beak. In 1968, the Hadrosaurus became the first ever mounted dinosaur.

This dinosaur was discovered in Haddonfield, New Jersey and the excavation site, known as the Hadrosaurus Foulkii Leidy Site, is now a National Historic Landmark. New Jersey has officially declared the Hadrosaurus as the state dinosaur and a sculpture now stands in the center of the town in Haddonfield commemorating its discovery.

Hypacrosaurus

How do I pronounce its name? High-pah-kroe-sore-uss

What does its name mean? The almost the top lizard.

How big were they? 30 feet/9 meters long and weighed 6000 lbs/3000 kg

What did they like to eat? Plants.

Where did they live? In the forest of North America.

Tell Me More

Living throughout the late Cretaceous period, Hypacrosaurus was a duck-billed dinosaur. Just like numerous other duckbills, Hypacrosaurus had a hollow crest located upon the top of its head. It is thought that these crests were actually used to produce loud horn blasts, which might have been heard from a good distance in order to alert the herd about approaching predators.

This duck-bill was known to possess a self sharpen teeth process. The front of Hypacrosaurus' mouth started with a toothless bill, followed by rows of self sharpening teeth found farther back in the mouth close to the animal's cheeks. The top teeth were set in the animal's mouth at a slant to the bottom teeth which made them grind against one another.

Kentrosaurus

How do I pronounce its name? ken-tro-SORE-us

What does its name mean? The spiked lizard.

How big were they? 16 feet/9 meters long and weighed 4000 lbs/1800 kg

What did they like to eat? Plants.

Where did they live? In the woodlands of eastern Africa.

Tell Me More

The Kentrosaurus, a spike tailed plant eater belonged to the late Jurassic period and was discovered in Tanzania. Kentrosaurus had dermal armor plates attached to its back; these plates little by little became narrower as they ran downward on its body until they were much more like spikes.

Their front legs were shorter compared to its back legs, not because it walked on two feet, but since it had to keep its head close to the ground to snack on low lying plants. Kentrosaurus may have been able to whirl its tail at fast speeds that would have made it possible for the sharp spikes on its tail to go through the flesh of predators.

Olorotitan

Gigantic Swan

How do I pronounce its name? oh-LOW-roe-tie-tan

What does its name mean? The gigantic swan.

How big were they? 40 feet/12 meters long and weighed 5500 lbs/2500 kg

What did they like to eat? Plants.

Where did they live? In the forest of eastern Russia.

Tell Me More

Existing during the late Cretaceous period, Olorotitan is Greek for "giant swan". Olorotitan gained its name for its rather long neck, compared with other types of duck-billed dinosaurs, in addition to the tall, massive hatchet like hollow crest decorating its head, which was most likely vibrantly colored to entice mates.

Uncovered in eastern Russia in 2003, Olorotitan is one of the most complete duck-billed dinosaur fossil ever to be discovered beyond North America. It's currently on exhibit at the Amur Museum of Natural History in the former U.S.S.R., you may desire to visit comrade.

Pachycephalosaurus

How do I pronounce its name? pack-ee-SEF-ah-low-SORE-us

What does its name mean? The thick-headed lizard.

How big were they? 18 feet/5.5 meters long and weighed 4000 lbs/1800 kg

What did they like to eat? Plants.

Where did they live? In the woodlands of North America.

Tell Me More

The thick domed skull of bone-headed dinosaur, Pachycephalosaurus, safeguarded the small braincase during the course of fighting. Flank butting, not actually head-butting, was probably what took place during battle since there is zero proof of scars or even injury on Pachyrhinosaurus heads. The bony dome discovered as being 10 inches thick and its' domes back area, edged with bony knobs and the short blunt spikes that protruded upwards from the snout, bestowed one of the most bizarre visual aspect to this bonehead.

The tiny jagged teeth were unable to chew on the hard, woody plants that were unique with the late Cretaceous period, which nourished other dinosaurs. It is believed that Pachycephalosaurus survived an eating plan of insects, leaves, seeds and fruit.

Pentaceratops

How do I pronounce its name? PENT-ah-ser-ah-tops

What does its name mean? The five-horned face.

How big were they? 25 feet/7.5 meters long and weighed 10000 lbs/4500 kg

What did they like to eat? Plants.

Where did they live? In the grasslands of western North America.

Tell Me More

In spite of the meaning of its own name "five-horned face", this particular dinosaur of the late Cretaceous period merely possessed three horns, two large ones over its eyes and a smaller sized one on the end of its snout. The two additional protrusions were actually outgrowths of the dinosaur's cheekbones, rather than true horns.

Just like other horned dinosaurs called ceratopsians, Pentaceratops had a parrot like beak, which it utilized to chop through plant substance and is generally thought that it possessed a row of teeth inside of its mouth. Pentaceratops had the greatest skull of any type of land animal to have ever existed. The majority of the enormous skull forms the long neck frill, extending from the tip of its beak to the top of its bony frill. Pentaceratops had the biggest head of any dinosaur, around 10 feet in length.

Phorusrhacos

Branch Holder

How do I pronounce its name? foe-roos-RAY-coss

What does its name mean? The branch holder.

How big were they? 8 feet/2.5 meters long and weighed 300 lbs/136 kg

What did they like to eat? Animals.

Where did they live? In the woodlands and grasslands of South America.

Tell Me More

Nicknamed the "Terror Bird" for obvious reasons, it was among the greatest meat eating birds to have ever existed. Considering its large size and clawed wings fashioned just like a meat hook for tackling prey, and a massive pulverizing beak, gave it a terrifying look.

Theorizing from the behavior of a very similar relative, the Kelenken, various scientists consider that the Terror Bird snatched its quivering lunch with its talons, and then bashed it repeatedly on the terrain to kill it. Phorusrhacos lived during the middle Miocene period.

Pteranodon

How do I pronounce its name? Tear-ANN-owe-don

What does its name mean? The no teeth.

How big were they? 20 feet/6 meters long and weighed 30 lbs/14 kg

What did they like to eat? Fish.

Where did they live? Around the coastlines of North America.

Tell Me More

This medium sized, late Cretaceous period pterosaur reached wingspans of approximately six feet, and its wings were actually composed of skin rather than feathers. Its additional bird like features consisted of webbed feet and a toothless beak.

Pteranodon, likewise known as Pterodactyl, were massive flying reptiles which lived around the coastline, and most likely preyed on critters which inhabited the sea, such as fish and squid. They possessed a long head crest that was possibly used to help counter balance the heaviness of its enormous beak.

Quetzalcoatlus

How do I pronounce its name? KETT-zal-coe-AT-luss

What does its name mean? The Mexican feathered god.

How big were they? 50 feet/15 meters long and weighed 440 lbs/200 kg

What did they like to eat? Fish and dead animals.

Where did they live? North America.

Tell Me More

Quetzalcoatlus are actually flying reptiles from the late Cretaceous period and are understood as being amongst the greatest flying creatures to have ever inhabited the Earth. Named after the terrifying Aztec god, this gigantic pterosaur achieved wingspans of more than 50 feet that could well be wider than a small aircraft.

They were most likely terrestrial stalkers, the same as nowadays stork, and quite possibly hunted small sized animals ashore or in small streams. Whenever up on the ground, Quetzalcoatlus would most likely use their fore and hind limbs in order to walk, while searching for food.

Sauroposeidon

Earthquake God Lizard

How do I pronounce its name? SORE-oh-poe-SIDE-on

What does its name mean? The earthquake god lizard.

How big were they? 112 ft/34 m long, 56 ft/17 m tall, and weighed 120,000 lbs/54,000 kg

What did they like to eat? Plants.

Where did they live? Forest of North America.

Tell Me More

This particular sauropod dinosaur from the early Cretaceous period is among the tallest herbivorous dinosaurs which ever existed. Due to its extraordinarily long neck, this dinosaur may well have extended above 56 feet into the air, skyscraping enough in order to peek into a sixth floor apartment window.

Sauroposeidon are additionally considered as being among the lengthiest and heaviest dinosaur.

Seismosaurus or Diplocaulus

Can You find the man?

Earth Shaking Lizard

How do I pronounce its name? SIZE-moe-SORE-us, or dip-LOW-doe-kuss

What does its name mean? The earth shaking lizard, or double beam.

How big were they? 115 ft/35 m long and weighed 200,000 lbs/91,000 kg

What did they like to eat? Plants.

Where did they live? Forest of southwestern North America.

Tell Me More

A nearly unimaginably massive animal, Seismosaurus lived during the late Jurassic period, a time when the Earth's warm temperatures stimulated rapid plant growth. This helped to insure a substantial source of food. Paleontologists believe they most likely utilized their comb like set of teeth to swiftly remove the leaves of close by trees, and gobbled them down without chewing.

The name Seismosaurus literally means "Earthquake Lizard," due to the fact that this dinosaur was without a doubt enormous enough that it may in fact, have shook the earth as it stepped.

Seismosaurus has become a deprecated genus, a dinosaur which was previously believed to be unique, but has since been revealed to belong to a previously existing genus. Originally regarded as the greatest of all dinosaurs, the majority of the scientists now agree that the house sized Seismosaurus was actually probably a species of Diplodocus. That's the reason why the two names are listed.

Spinosaurus

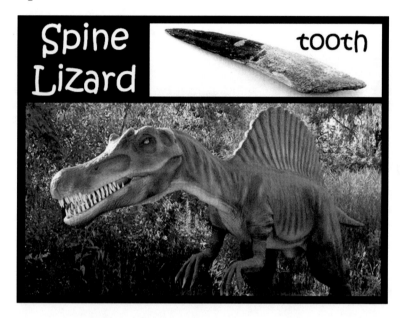

How do I pronounce its name? SPY-nuh-SAWR-us

What does its name mean? The spine lizard.

How big were they? 40 ft/12 m long, 14 ft/4 m tall and weighed 14,000 lbs/6,350 kg

What did they like to eat? Animals and fish.

Where did they live? The marshlands of North Africa.

Tell Me More

Living in amidst the tidal flats and watercourses of northern Africa, Spinosaurus was definitely an eater of fish even though it may have scavenged carcasses when the opportunity arose. Equipped with a long slender snout and serrated straight teeth, 12 on each side of the upper jaw, was utilized to catch fish. Many paleontologists consider that Spinosaurus was a scavenger, making use of its alligator shaped mouth in order to snack on the soft flesh of rotting animal carcasses.

Distinguished for the long neural spines upon its backside which grew more than 5 feet long made this amongst the largest theropods from the middle Cretaceous period, the skin sail or hump may well have been utilized for energy storage, courtship displays or perhaps regulation of heat.

The Spinosaurus was actually even larger sized than the T- Rex and may well have been the biggest meat eating dinosaur ever.

Stegosaurus

How do I pronounce its name? Steg –oh- SOR- us

What does its name mean? The roof lizard.

How big were they? 30 ft/9 m long, 14 ft/4 m tall and weighed 15,000 lbs/6,800 kg

What did they like to eat? Animals and fish.

Where did they live? The forest of western North America and Europe.

Tell Me More

Stegosaurus was a huge, plant eating dinosaur which inhabited North America and Europe (Portugal), during the late Jurassic period. Exactly what made this herbivore particularly eye-catching were the double rows of massive, bony plates jutting out from its backside. Nobody is actually completely sure why Stegosaurus possessed these types of plates, they may have evolved for defensive purposes due to the fact that there were certainly hungry predators about like the T-Rex and Allosaurus, or perhaps they may have functioned to dissipate heat from this dinosaur's body, the same as the ears on an elephant.

Trackways of Stegosaurus reveal that it was a herd animal with every age of animals living with each other. This herd way of thinking would certainly have provided protection from predators for the defenseless, smaller youngsters. Although a younger Stegosaurus possessed just the same physical characteristics of an adult in a smaller scale, it is certainly not conceivable that it would have had the ability to defend itself from Allosaurus, the big meat eater of its time.

The tail spikes of Stegosaurus were certainly used for defense against Allosaurus! Fossil evidence reveals a pierced Allosaurus tail vertebra into which a Stegosaurus tail spike fitted into flawlessly.

Stygimoloch

Demon from the River of Death

How do I pronounce its name? stih-gee-MOLE-lock

What does its name mean? The Styx Demon- demon from the river of death.

How big were they? 10 feet/9 meters long and weighed 200 lbs/90 kg

What did they like to eat? Plants.

Where did they live? The forest of western North America and Europe.

Tell Me More

Alive throughout the late Cretaceous period, Stygimoloch was known for its clusters of spikes on the rear about the head, wherein a long main horn is encircled by 2 or 3 smaller horns, and a tall slender dome.

Being a part of the boneheaded family of dinosaurs and appearing like a demon, this particular dinosaur was called Stygimoloch, which means "Styx Demon." The River Styx separated the Earth from Hades in Greek Mythology.

Even though appearing very scary, the Stygimoloch was most likely fairly harmless, feasting on plants and leaving other dinosaurs alone.

Styracosaurus

How do I pronounce its name? STY-rack-oh-SORE-us

What does its name mean? The spiked lizard.

How big were they? 18 feet/5.5 meters long and weighed 6000 lbs/2700 kg

What did they like to eat? Plants.

Where did they live? The forest of North America.

Tell Me More

Living close to the end of the age of the dinosaurs, the late Cretaceous period, Styrocosaurus is among the most intriguing of all the horned dinosaurs. Their head was massive, with large nostrils, a flat face extending upward into a massive frill, which was itself crowned by no less than six treacherous spikes.

As though all of that weren't enough, this plant eater had a horn prolonged from its snout two feet long, and two smaller horns jutting out from its cheeks. Plus the Styrocosaurus possessed a beak like a bird, and shearing cheek teeth used for slicing plants.

The spikes on the horned dinosaur would certainly have bestowed it a scary appearance and could have inflicted terrific damage on a predator if attacked.

Therizinosaurs

How do I pronounce its name? THER-ih-ZINE-oh-SORE-us

What does its name mean? The reaping lizard.

How big were they? 40 feet/12 meters long and weighed 12,000 lbs/5400 kg

What did they like to eat? Plants.

Where did they live? The forest of western North America and Asia.

Tell Me More

Theizinosaurus is one of the weirdest dinosaurs to have ever lived. It is a descendent of the meat eating dinosaurs known as theropods, however it most likely did not eat meat. Rather, Theizinosaurus made use of its long claws to rake vegetation into its mouth. These claws were the size of human arms, around two feet in length. Additionally it possessed a beak like a bird, a long neck, and stood upright on its two hind legs.

Occupying during the late Cretaceous period, paleontologists believe those funny looking long claws were excellent for gathering fruits and leaves, similar to a modern day sloth.

Troodon

How do I pronounce its name? TRUE-oh-don

What does its name mean? The wounding tooth.

How big were they? 7 feet/2 meters long and weighed 100 lbs/45 kg

What did they like to eat? Small animals.

Where did they live? The grasslands of western North America and Asia.

Tell Me More

Troodon were from the late Cretaceous period and little according to dinosaur standards. However, they might possibly have been just one of the smartest dinosaurs ever, due to the fact that they had the largest known brain of any dinosaur, in comparison to their body size.

Even though not actually a very big theropod, it is thought that Troodon was certainly an effective hunter due to very long, slender hind limbs, indicating that these creatures had the ability to run swiftly. They had sizeable, retractable sickle fashioned claws on the second toes and huge eyes which suggest good vision.

Tropeognathus

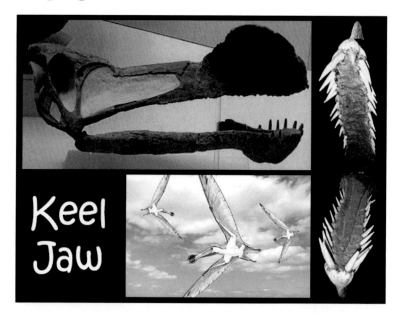

How do I pronounce its name? Trop-ee-og-NAY-thus

What does its name mean? The keel jaw.

How big were they? 27 feet/8 meters long and weighed 100 lbs/45 kg

What did they like to eat? Fish.

Where did they live? The coastlands of western Europe and South America.

Tell Me More

Tropeognathus was actually uncovered in South America. It thrived near coastal waters during the late Cretaceous period, where it hunted fish and other creatures inhabiting the shallow waters. Recognized for their keel tipped or crested snouts, which may have been utilized to crack the shells of shellfishes. This particular pterosaur was huge with wingspans reaching out to 27 feet wide.

Tyrannosaurus Rex

How do I pronounce its name? tie-RAN-oh-SORE-us REX

What does its name mean? The tyrant lizard king.

How big were they? 40 feet/12 meters long and weighed 14,000 lbs/6350 kg

What did they like to eat? Large animals.

Where did they live? The woodlands and marshes of North America.

Tell Me More

As the last great carnivore of the Cretaceous period, Tyrannosaurus Rex, nick named T-Rex, was an efficient killing machine stalking the North American landscape. With a specially strengthened nose structure which enabled it to deliver bone splintering, crushing chomps to both caught prey and during the course of fighting with others of its species, a T-Rex lower jaw could supply 10,000 newtons of pressure, the equivalent of having the ability to raise a semi-trailer.

The staring theropod of many movies, books, video games and television shows, T-Rex was undoubtedly a terrifying hunter with a remarkable sense of smell. Averaging 13 feet tall at the hips, equipped with two very powerful forelimbs which bore two claws on each, and a huge head (up to 5 feet long), enormous enough to gobble a man whole!

The largest sized tooth found of any meat eating dinosaur is that of a T-Rex. It is estimated to have been around 12inches long.

Velociraptor

How do I pronounce its name? vel-OSS-ih-rap-tore

What does its name mean? The swift seizer.

How big were they? 6 feet/2 meters long and weighed 65 lbs/30 kg

What did they like to eat? Small animals.

Where did they live? The forest of Asia.

Tell Me More

Velociraptor is most likely amongst the more famous dinosaurs that ever existed, second only to the T-Rex. It reached its fame through the box office hit titled "Jurassic Park." In this particular movie, Velociraptor's size was enhanced to make it appear scarier. Velociraptors were vicious, but they were likewise very little and it's unlikely a 35 pound feathered raptor reminiscent of a gigantic chicken would have elicited all that excitement at the theater.

Velociraptor lived in the late Cretaceous period and while a small dinosaur had extremely effective weapons for killing prey. A sizeable sickle shaped claw, over 2 inches long, was positioned on each hind foot. Putting to use these enlarged claws, they would bounce onto their prey ripping away with the slashing weapons.

Among the more famous dinosaur fossils ever discovered features a Velociraptor in the center of combat along with a Protoceratops.

Cretaceous Footprint

Alvis Delk Print
in the Sir George Series

Photo: David Lines, Creation Evidence Museum

Human Footprint with Dino Track

It's been commonly thought throughout the scientific community that man did not exist during the same time period as the dinosaurs. This is because the conventional geologic timetable demonstrates that people did not live until over 60 million years after dinosaurs became extinct.

However, in recent years that thinking has been challenged. In July of 2000, the discovery of a fossil footprint unearthed in the State of Texas, in North America has raised many questions. This fossil is of an 11 inch human footprint intruded by an Acrocanthosaurus dinosaur print. After being examined by an independent professional laboratory with X-ray scans, it clearly showed both human and dinosaur prints, removing the possibility of the footprints being faked or carved. This raises more questions for paleontologists, and hopefully answers will be found. For more information on this footprint fossil and its discovery go to http://www.creationevidence.org or http://bit.ly/16fnKDC for the footprint.

What Did You Learn Today? Questions

1. What does a Sauropod dinosaur like to eat?

2. What dinosaur shares characteristics with the modern day crocodile?

3. Does the funny looking pot bellied Beipiaosaurs eat other dinosaurs?

4. What dinosaur was considered "built like a tank" because of all its armor?

5. This meat eating giant was even bigger than T-Rex, what is his name?

6. The duck-billed dinosaur Hadrosaurus, became the first ever mounted dinosaur skeleton. True or False?

7. This duck billed dinosaur was thought to make loud horn blast sounds? True or False?

8. Did the "spikey" Kentrosaurus live in Africa or North America?

9. This dinosaur's name means "Gigantic Swan", what is its name?

10. You could say that the Pachycephalosaurus was a real bonehead, because he belonged to what dinosaur family?

11. The five horned face or Pentaceratops dinosaur had the largest skull or beak, of any land animal?

12. My name is Phorusrhacos, and it means branch holder, what is my nickname?

13. My name is Pteranodon, and it's pronounced "tear-Ann-owe-don", which means, no "what"?

14. Quetzalcoatlus is the largest flying dinosaur with wingspans wider than a small airplane, reaching up to 50 feet. True or False?

15. The Sauroposeidon was the tallest dinosaur ever; it was so tall it could have looked into a sixth floor apartment window. True or False?

16. What dinosaurs' name means "Earth Shaking Lizard" or "Earthquake Lizard" because it may have shook the ground as it walked?

17. Did the Spinosaurus like to eat animals and fish around the marshlands of Florida?

18. The Stegosaurus was an herbivore, which means he liked to eat what?

19. It may be boneheaded, but the Stygimoloch, whose name means "Styx Demon – Demon from the River of Death" liked to eat plants. True or False?

20. The Styrocosaurus had a beak like a bird, which helped it eat meat. True or False?

21. The weird looking Theizinosaurus had eating habits like a modern day sloth, and had two foot long, funny looking what?

22. I'm considered to be one of the smartest dinosaurs ever, and my name means "wounding tooth". What is my name?

23. The flying reptile Tropeognathus, which lived around coastlands, liked to eat fish. True or False?

24. The Tyrannosaurus Rex was one of the most powerful dinosaurs; its name means "Tyrant Lizard King", what is its nickname?

25. The Velociraptor had very effective weapons for killing prey. Was it two inch long claws, or two inch long horns?

26. The "Cretaceous Footprint" fossil discovered in July of 2000 has two footprints in it. One footprint is from a dinosaur, what is the other footprint from?

Grrrrr...

What Did You Learn Today? Answers

1. Plants.

2. The Baryonyx.

3. No, they eat plants.

4. The Euoplocephalus.

5. Giganotosaurus.

6. True.

7. The Hypacrosaurus.

8. Africa.

9. Olorotitan.

10. The boneheaded dinosaurs.

11. Skull.

12. Terror Bird

13. No teeth, because of my toothless beak.

14. False, dinosaurs do NOT fly. Quetzalcoatlus was a flying reptile.

15. True.

16. Seismosaurus.

17. No, it liked to eat them around the marshlands of North Africa.

18. Plants.

19. True.

20. False, it did have a beak though, which helped it eat plants.

21. Claws.

22. Troodon, because they had the largest known brain of any dinosaur in comparison to their body size.

23. True.

24. T-Rex.

25. Its two inch long claws.

26. Human footprint.

Ahrrrr...!!!

Enjoyed the Book?

Thank you for buying this book. I hope that you and your children enjoy reading the book and learning about the animals in the book as much as I did writing it. If you found the book enjoyable, please help me out by posting a review on the Amazon page. Thank you for taking the time to do so. It is very much appreciated.

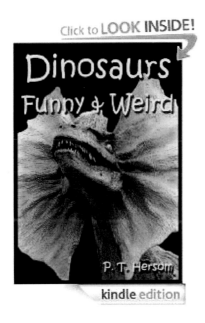

Leave a Dinosaurs Funny & Weird review

http://amzn.to/12Ov2Zw

Other Books to Enjoy by P. T. Hersom

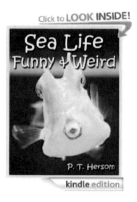

Sea Life Funny & Weird Marine Animals

http://amzn.to/15QEYoJ

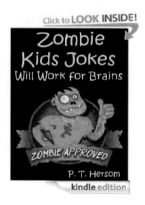

Zombie Jokes: Will Work for Brains http://amzn.to/13pR0mU

Zombie Party Ideas for Kids: How to Party Like a Zombie

http://amzn.to/14uwDo7

Dinosaurs Funny & Weird Extinct Animals

By P. T. Hersom

First Published, 2013

Printed in the United States of America

Hersom House Publishing

3365 NE 45th St, Suite 101, Ocala, Florida 34479

49355220R00043

Made in the USA
San Bernardino, CA
22 May 2017